MW01169277

MELANIE MARTINEZ:

Dreams, Music, and Magic–How a
Young Dreamer Turned Her Music
into Magic

Gary A. Robinson

Copyright © Gary A. Robinson,2024

All rights reserved. No part of this publication may be reproduced or transmitted in any form or by any means including photocopying, recording or other electronic or mechanical methods without the prior written permission of the publisher except in the case of brief quotations embodied in critical reviews and certain other non-commercial uses permitted by copyright law.

TABLE OF CONTENTS

INTRODUCTION

Imagine a world where your dreams can turn into songs, your imagination can come to life, and you can be exactly who you want to be. That's the kind of magical world Melanie Martinez creates through her music, videos, and stories. But Melanie's journey didn't start with magic, it started with a dream.

Born on April 28, 1995, in New York, Melanie was a curious and creative child who loved expressing herself in different ways. Whether it was singing, drawing, or writing, she always found unique ways to show the world who she was. From a young age, Melanie dreamed of sharing her music with others. Little did she know that one day, her voice would touch millions of hearts around the world!

As a child, Melanie was a little shy but had big dreams. She didn't always know how to fit in at school, but she found comfort in her creativity. When she sang or made art, Melanie felt free. She knew she was different, but she also knew that being different was something special. She wanted to create music that would speak to people who felt like they didn't quite fit in, just like her.

Melanie's love for music grew as she got older. She would sing at home, at school, and anywhere she could! She also started learning how to play the guitar, which became another way for her to share her feelings through songs. Melanie knew she had something special to offer, but like all big dreams, her journey wasn't always easy. She faced challenges along the way, and sometimes things didn't go as planned. But Melanie never gave up on her dream of becoming a singer and telling her stories through music.

When Melanie was just a teenager, she got a big chance to share her voice with the world. She auditioned for a popular TV show called The Voice in 2012. This was a huge opportunity for Melanie, and she was nervous! But she stood on that stage and sang her heart out. To her surprise, all of the celebrity coaches turned their chairs around, meaning they wanted her on their team! Melanie chose Adam Levine, the lead singer of Maroon 5, to be her coach.

Even though Melanie didn't win The Voice, her journey was far from over. In fact, it was just beginning. Melanie realized that while the show gave her a chance to shine, she wanted to be more than just a singer. She wanted to create her own world through music, one where her imagination could run wild. So, she started writing her own songs, creating her own unique style that no one had ever heard before. She combined music, art, and storytelling in a way that made her stand out from everyone else.

In 2015, Melanie released her very first album called Cry Baby. But this wasn't just any ordinary album, it told a special story about a girl named Cry Baby, who was a lot like Melanie. Through the songs on the album, Melanie shared feelings of being different, feeling lost, and learning to be strong. Fans everywhere loved Cry Baby and connected with her story. Melanie's music videos for the songs were filled with colorful, imaginative scenes that looked like they came straight out of a dream!

Melanie didn't stop there. She continued to create more music, more art, and more stories that inspire kids and adults alike to follow their dreams and be themselves. Her creativity knows no limits, and she shows everyone that even the biggest dreams can come true if you believe in yourself.

So, what makes Melanie Martinez so special? It's her ability to turn her dreams into music and her music into magic! Through this book, you'll discover how Melanie went from a little girl with big dreams to a pop star who makes her own rules. You'll learn about her challenges, her victories, and how she continues to inspire young dreamers everywhere to never stop believing in the power of their imagination.

Let's take a magical journey together and explore the amazing world of Melanie Martinez, where music and dreams come together to create something truly magical!

Chapter 1: A Creative Spark

Every big dream starts with a little spark, and for Melanie Martinez, that spark was her imagination. From the time she was a young girl, Melanie was always full of creative ideas. She didn't just see the world around her as it was, she saw it as it could be, full of color, music, and magic. Whether it was drawing, singing, or telling stories, Melanie's imagination was always working, turning ordinary things into something special.

Growing up in Baldwin, New York, Melanie loved spending time at home, where she could express herself freely. While some kids were busy playing games or sports, Melanie was busy creating. She loved to draw pictures, write poems, and make up songs. Art and music became her way of showing the world who she was, even when she couldn't find the right words to say.

When she wasn't busy creating her own little world at home, Melanie loved listening to music. Her parents played all kinds of music, from hip-hop to pop, and Melanie soaked it all in like a sponge. She loved the way music made her feel, it was like the songs were telling stories, just like the ones she made up in her head. Melanie wanted to be a part of that magical world of music, where she could tell her own stories and share them with others.

One of the first things Melanie realized about herself was that she didn't always fit in with other kids at school. She was a little shy, and she felt different from the people around her. But instead of letting that make her feel sad, Melanie used her creativity to feel strong. She would spend hours at home, drawing pictures and writing songs that made her feel happy and free. Art and music became her safe place, where she could be exactly who she wanted to be without worrying about what others thought.

Melanie's creativity didn't stop at drawing or writing. She also loved to perform. At family gatherings, she would put on little shows, singing and dancing for her relatives. It was during these moments that Melanie discovered something important: she loved making people smile with her creativity. Even though she was shy, performing gave her the chance to connect with others and share her imaginative world. That feeling sparked something inside her, a dream to one day perform on a much bigger stage.

But Melanie's creativity wasn't just about being fun. It was also a way for her to deal with her feelings. When she felt sad or confused, she would turn to her art or her music to express those emotions. Instead of keeping her feelings bottled up, she found ways to let them out through her creativity. This helped her feel better and also made her realize that music and art could help others feel better too.

As Melanie grew older, she knew that she wanted to do something big with her creativity. She didn't just want to keep her songs and stories to herself, she wanted to share them with the world. She dreamed of becoming a singer, someone who could inspire others with her unique voice and imaginative ideas. And though she didn't know exactly how she would get there, Melanie's creative spark kept her moving forward, dreaming big, and working hard to make her dreams come true.

That creative spark inside Melanie was the beginning of her amazing journey. It was the start of something magical, something that would take her from a shy little girl with big dreams to a pop star who could bring her imagination to life through her music. But as Melanie would soon find out, the road to success was full of twists and turns, challenges and surprises. And through it all, her creativity and determination would help her turn every dream into reality.

Chapter 2: Singing to the Stars

Melanie Martinez always had a special connection to music, even as a little girl. She would hum tunes, sing along to her favorite songs, and make up her own melodies. It wasn't long before everyone around her could see that Melanie's voice was something special. But for Melanie, singing wasn't just about sounding good, it was about expressing herself, sharing her emotions, and telling stories in a way that only music could do.

As she grew older, Melanie's love for music only deepened. She would listen to artists like Britney Spears, The Beatles, and Shakira, who all had their own unique styles. Melanie admired how they could create entire worlds through their music. She wanted to do the same. She didn't just want to sing; she wanted to share her story with the world in a way that was completely her own.

By the time she reached high school, Melanie had begun to take her singing more seriously. She knew she had a dream to chase, and that dream was to become a singer. But it wasn't always easy. Melanie was shy, and standing in front of people to sing made her nervous. Still, she never let her fear stop her. She practiced singing every day, sometimes alone in her room, and sometimes in front of her family and friends. Slowly but surely, she began to find her confidence.

Melanie's big break came in 2012 when she was just 17 years old. She decided to audition for a popular singing competition on TV called The Voice. This was a huge moment for Melanie. Not only was it a chance to show the world her voice, but it was also a big step outside her comfort zone. Singing in front of her family was one thing, but singing on national television was a whole different experience! Despite the nerves, Melanie was determined to give it her best shot.

On the day of her audition, Melanie stepped onto the stage with her guitar, her heart racing. She was about to sing in front of celebrity judges and millions of viewers watching at home. The lights were bright, and the audience was silent. Then, Melanie began to sing a hauntingly beautiful version of "Toxic" by Britney Spears. Her voice was soft yet powerful, filled with emotion. As she sang, the audience listened closely, and soon enough, something incredible happened: all four judges turned their chairs around, signaling that they wanted Melanie on their team!

It was a moment that Melanie would never forget. All four celebrity coaches Adam Levine, Blake Shelton, CeeLo Green, and Christina Aguilera were impressed by her unique voice and style. Melanie chose Adam Levine, the lead singer of Maroon 5, to be her coach. She had taken a huge leap of faith, and it paid off in the most amazing way. For the first time, Melanie felt like her dream of becoming a singer was within reach.

Though Melanie didn't win The Voice, her time on the show changed everything. It gave her the confidence she needed to pursue her music career. More importantly, it showed her that her voice was unique and that people were listening. She realized that she didn't need to sound like anyone else, she just needed to be herself.

After the show, Melanie knew that her journey wasn't over. In fact, it had just begun. She started writing her own songs, crafting her own sound, and imagining a world where her music could tell stories that no one else was telling. She was determined to use her voice not just to sing, but to create a magical world where her fans could escape, dream, and feel understood.

Melanie's time on The Voice wasn't the end of her story, it was just the beginning of something truly magical. She had sung to the stars, and now she was ready to bring those stars back down to Earth, turning them into songs that would light up the world. From this point on, Melanie's voice would be her superpower, and her dreams were about to get even bigger.

Chapter 3: The Voice Adventure

Melanie Martinez's journey on The Voice was like stepping into a whole new world, a world filled with excitement, challenges, and the chance to make her dreams come true. At just 17 years old, Melanie decided to take a leap of faith and audition for the popular TV show. It was a big decision for her because she had always been shy and nervous about performing in front of large crowds. But something inside her told her that this was her moment, her chance to share her voice with the world.

The year was 2012, and The Voice was one of the most-watched singing competitions on TV. Talented singers from all over the country would audition for a spot on the show, hoping to impress four celebrity coaches Adam Levine, Blake Shelton, Christina Aguilera, and CeeLo Green. Melanie knew that she wasn't just competing against other singers; she was trying to stand out among thousands of talented performers.

When the day of her audition came, Melanie was filled with nervous energy. She clutched her guitar tightly as she stepped onto the big stage. The lights were bright, and the audience was silent, waiting to hear her voice. The four coaches sat with their backs to her, and it was up to Melanie to make them turn their chairs around, which meant they liked what they heard.

Melanie chose to sing "Toxic" by Britney Spears, a song she loved because of its unique sound and edgy vibe. But she didn't just sing the song the way everyone had heard it before she made it her own. With her soft, haunting voice, she played her guitar and delivered a version of the song that was completely different from anything the audience or the coaches had expected.

As she sang, Melanie poured her heart into every note. She didn't just want to impress the judges, she wanted to share a part of herself with them. And then, one by one, something amazing happened: the coaches started turning their chairs around! Adam Levine was the first to turn, followed by CeeLo Green and Blake Shelton. Finally, Christina Aguilera turned her chair, making it a full four-chair turn. All of the celebrity coaches wanted Melanie on their team!

For Melanie, this moment was a dream come true. She had stepped onto that stage filled with nerves, but she left feeling like she had finally found her place. The judges were impressed with her unique voice and style, and she had proven that she could stand out from the crowd. Now, the next step was to choose which coach she wanted to guide her through the competition. After thinking it over, Melanie made the big decision to join Adam Levine's team. She admired his talent and felt like he understood the kind of artist she wanted to become.

With Adam as her coach, Melanie entered the next stage of The Voice, the battle rounds. This part of the competition was tough because it meant singing against another contestant in a duet. The coaches had to choose who would stay and who would go home. Melanie faced her first battle with nerves but didn't let them stop her from giving it her all. She and her duet partner performed a beautiful rendition of "Lights" by Ellie Goulding, and once again, Melanie's unique voice and style stood out. Adam chose Melanie to continue in the competition.

As the competition went on, Melanie faced more challenges. Each round brought new songs, new performances, and new pressure to do her best. Melanie knew that every performance was a chance to share more of herself with the audience, and she never held back. She sang with emotion, creativity, and a style that was all her own.

Although Melanie didn't make it all the way to the final round of The Voice, her journey on the show was a huge success. She had won over millions of fans with her voice and her unique personality. More importantly, she had discovered something about herself; she didn't need to sound like anyone else or follow anyone else's path. Melanie was ready to carve her own path in the music world, one that was full of imagination and creativity.

After her time on The Voice ended, Melanie knew that this was just the beginning of her adventure. She had learned so much from the experience, and now she was ready to take everything she had learned and put it into her own music. She didn't just want to be a singer, she wanted to be an artist who created a world that people could get lost in. With the support of her growing fan base, Melanie was ready to take the next step on her journey toward making her dreams a reality.

The adventure of The Voice had taught Melanie one important lesson: never be afraid to be yourself. Even in the face of nerves, pressure, and competition, she stayed true to her unique voice and style. And that's what made her stand out not just on the show, but in the world of music.

Chapter 4: Making Her Own Path

After her unforgettable experience on The Voice, Melanie Martinez knew she had to carve her own unique path in the music world. The competition had been an incredible journey, but now it was time for her to take everything she had learned and put it into practice. She was ready to create music that reflected her individuality, creativity, and the stories she wanted to share with the world.

With her heart set on making her own mark, Melanie began writing songs that came straight from her soul. No longer confined by the expectations of others, she felt free to explore her emotions and experiences. Each song became a piece of her story, a way for her to connect with her fans on a deeper level. Melanie poured her heart into her lyrics, crafting songs that spoke about love, heartbreak, and the struggles of being a young woman trying to find her place in the world.

One of the most exciting things for Melanie was the chance to experiment with her sound. She didn't want to be just another pop singer, she wanted to create a unique musical style that combined different genres, including pop, alternative, and even a hint of theatrical flair. This vision of her music was inspired by her love for storytelling, art, and fashion. She wanted to create songs that felt like vivid stories, drawing listeners into a world filled with imagination.

Melanie also wanted to create a strong visual identity that matched her music. She began to develop a unique style that blended vintage aesthetics with a modern twist. Bright colors, playful outfits, and whimsical themes became part of her brand. Her fashion sense was just as expressive as her music, and she knew that the two needed to go hand in hand. This creative vision led her to think about how her music videos could enhance her songs, adding another layer of storytelling and creativity.

As she continued to write and develop her style, Melanie knew it was time to record her first album. In 2015, she released her debut album, Cry Baby, which would become a significant turning point in her career. The album was a reflection of her journey, showcasing her unique voice and artistic vision. It told the story of a character named Cry Baby, who represented Melanie's own experiences of feeling misunderstood and different from others. Through Cry Baby, Melanie wanted to show her fans that it's okay to be different and that everyone has their struggles.

With hits like "Dollhouse" and "Pity Party," Cry Baby quickly gained attention and love from fans around the world. The songs were catchy, relatable, and filled with emotion, resonating with listeners who felt the same way Melanie had felt. She poured her heart into every track, crafting music that spoke to the experiences of young people everywhere. It wasn't just about the music; it was about creating a safe space for her fans to feel understood and accepted.

The success of Cry Baby propelled Melanie into the spotlight, but she was determined to stay true to herself. While many artists might have felt pressure to conform to industry standards, Melanie was resolute in her desire to create music that felt authentic to her. She wasn't just following trends; she was setting them. Melanie understood that her individuality was her superpower, and she wasn't afraid to embrace it.

One of the most important lessons Melanie learned during this time was the value of perseverance. The music industry can be challenging, and filled with ups and downs, but Melanie never wavered in her commitment to her art. She knew that making her own path meant facing obstacles, but she was determined to rise above them. She surrounded herself with a supportive team who believed in her vision, helping her navigate the music world while staying true to her artistic integrity.

As Cry Baby gained popularity, Melanie began to connect with her fans on social media, sharing snippets of her life, her music, and her creative process. She encouraged her followers to embrace their individuality, reminding them that they didn't have to fit into anyone else's mold. Melanie wanted everyone to know that it's perfectly okay to be different, and she hoped to inspire her fans to follow their dreams, just as she had followed hers.

Making her own path wasn't always easy, but Melanie's determination, creativity, and passion for music allowed her to forge ahead. She learned that success wasn't just about fame or recognition; it was about staying true to herself and creating art that made a difference. Through her journey, Melanie Martinez became a beacon of inspiration for young dreamers everywhere, showing them that with hard work, authenticity, and a little bit of magic, they too could create their own paths and turn their dreams into reality.

Chapter 5: Cry Baby's World

With the release of her debut album, Cry Baby, Melanie Martinez invited fans into a vivid and enchanting universe, one that was entirely her own. This world was filled with imagination, creativity, and powerful emotions. "Cry Baby" wasn't just a title; it was a character that represented the experiences of feeling different, misunderstood, and emotionally complex. Through this character, Melanie created a safe haven where people could explore their feelings and find comfort in knowing they weren't alone.

In Cry Baby's world, everything was beautifully whimsical yet profoundly relatable. Each song was like a chapter in a storybook, and together they painted a picture of a young girl navigating the complexities of growing up. The songs explored themes of love, heartbreak, and self-acceptance, inviting listeners to join Cry Baby on her journey. Whether it was the playful tones of "Dollhouse," where she explored the idea of perfection versus reality, or the powerful anthem "Pity Party," where she expressed feelings of loneliness and rejection, every track was an opportunity for fans to connect with their emotions.

The creativity didn't stop with the music. Melanie transformed her album into a multi-sensory experience. Each music video was a mini-movie that further brought Cry Baby's world to life. In these videos, she used vibrant colors, imaginative sets, and symbolic imagery to create a visual narrative that complemented her songs. For example, in the "Dollhouse" music video, the set resembled a toy house where everything appeared perfect on the outside but hid a darker reality inside. This powerful imagery resonated with fans who could relate to the feelings of wanting to appear perfect while dealing with inner struggles.

The album's artwork also played a crucial role in establishing Cry Baby's world. Melanie designed the cover to feature her as the character Cry Baby, complete with big, expressive eyes and a soft, innocent expression. This visual representation perfectly captured the essence of her character, a girl who may seem fragile but has a heart full of strength. The colorful, cartoonish design invited fans to step into her world and explore the emotional landscape she had created.

One of the most significant aspects of Cry Baby's world was its ability to promote self-acceptance and understanding. Melanie encouraged her fans to embrace their emotions, whether they felt happy, sad, or everything in between. She wanted to create a space where people could feel comfortable expressing themselves, no matter what they were going through. Through her music, Melanie showed her listeners that it's okay to be vulnerable, to feel deeply, and to express those feelings in whatever way feels right for them.

As her fan base grew, so did the impact of Cry Baby's world. Fans began to identify with the characters and the messages embedded in the songs. They found solace in Melanie's lyrics, often sharing their own stories of heartbreak and triumph. The connection between Melanie and her fans became a beautiful tapestry of shared experiences, reminding everyone that they weren't alone in their struggles.

Melanie also engaged with her fans directly, encouraging them to share their interpretations of Cry Baby's world through art, stories, and social media. This collaborative spirit created a sense of community among her followers, transforming Cry Baby's world into a collective experience. Fans felt empowered to express their emotions and creativity, inspired by Melanie's authenticity.

As the Cry Baby album continued to gain popularity, Melanie embarked on her first major tour, aptly named the Cry Baby Tour. This was an opportunity for her to bring the world of Cry Baby to life in front of her fans. The tour featured elaborate stage designs, costumes, and choreography that reflected the whimsical yet poignant nature of her music. Each performance was like a theatrical experience, allowing her fans to step into the magical universe she had created.

During the concerts, Melanie shared not just her songs but also her story, reminding her audience that the journey of self-discovery is ongoing. She encouraged them to embrace their uniqueness and never shy away from expressing their emotions. The energy in the arenas was electric, with fans singing along to every word, feeling seen and understood through the magic of Melanie's music.

In the end, Cry Baby's world was more than just an album; it was a celebration of creativity, emotion, and authenticity. It was a place where everyone could feel accepted for who they were, and where the magic of music brought people together. Through Cry Baby, Melanie Martinez created a universe that transcended boundaries, inspiring countless fans to find their own voices and embrace the beauty of their emotional journeys. With each song, each video, and each performance, Melanie invited her fans to join her on a journey of self-discovery, reminding them that it's okay to be a little different and that true magic lies in being unapologetically yourself.

Chapter 6: Dreams and Music Come Alive

As Melanie Martinez continued to grow as an artist, her dreams and music began to intertwine in beautiful and unexpected ways. With the success of her debut album Cry Baby, she was no longer just a girl with a dream she was becoming a prominent voice in the music industry, and her unique style was captivating audiences around the world. But for Melanie, this journey was about more than just fame; it was about making her dreams come alive through the power of music.

After the whirlwind of the Cry Baby Tour, Melanie felt a surge of inspiration. Performing live in front of her fans ignited a fire within her. Each concert was a celebration, a moment where she could connect with her audience and share the stories that mattered most to her. The energy of the crowd, the bright lights, and the sound of thousands of voices singing along fueled her creativity. It was during these performances that Melanie realized how music had the ability to create a magical atmosphere where dreams truly came alive.

But the dream didn't stop at just performing. Melanie wanted to keep evolving as an artist and explore new dimensions of her music. After the success of Cry Baby, she began writing new songs that delved even deeper into her emotions and experiences. She found herself drawing inspiration from her own life, her dreams, and even her fantasies. Every melody, lyric, and beat was a reflection of her journey, capturing moments of joy, sadness, love, and everything in between.

One of the most exciting parts of this creative process was collaborating with other talented artists and producers. Melanie sought out people who shared her vision and passion for music, and together they crafted sounds that blended different genres and styles. The result was a fresh and innovative approach to her work, allowing her to explore new musical territories while staying true to her unique identity.

In 2019, Melanie released her highly anticipated sophomore album, K-12. This concept album took her creative vision to new heights. It was not just a collection of songs; it was an entire experience that combined music, film, and art.

The album followed the story of a character named Cry Baby as she navigated the challenges of school and adolescence. Each song represented a different chapter in Cry Baby's journey, tackling issues like self-discovery, friendship, and the pressures of society.

But what truly made K-12 come alive was the accompanying film that Melanie wrote, directed, and produced. The film brought her music to life in a whole new way, showcasing vibrant visuals, intricate choreography, and powerful storytelling. Melanie wanted to create a world where her fans could escape reality and immerse themselves in the dreams and struggles of Cry Baby. The film premiered at the renowned Regency Village Theatre in Los Angeles, and fans from all over gathered to experience the magic together.

As Melanie's music and film came together, her dreams began to take flight. The release of K-12 not only showcased her talents as a musician but also highlighted her skills as a storyteller and filmmaker. She was no longer just a singer; she had become a multifaceted artist, using her platform to express herself in various creative ways. The combination of music and visual storytelling allowed her to connect with her audience on a deeper level, and her fans embraced this new direction with open arms.

Through the ups and downs of her journey, Melanie never lost sight of the importance of dreams. She often shared with her fans that following your passion and believing in yourself are essential ingredients for making those dreams come true. Her story served as a reminder that dreams are not just fantasies; they can become a reality if you work hard, stay true to yourself, and never stop believing.

As she continued to tour and promote K-12, Melanie made it a point to engage with her fans more intimately. She wanted them to feel like they were part of her journey. Whether it was through social media, meet-and-greet events, or fan interactions during her concerts, Melanie encouraged her supporters to share their dreams, stories, and experiences. She wanted to create a community where everyone felt valued and heard, reminding them that their dreams mattered just as much as hers.

In every performance, every song, and every film, Melanie Martinez brought her dreams to life. She transformed her aspirations into something tangible, using music as her canvas to express her innermost thoughts and feelings. Her journey was a testament to the power of creativity and the magic that happens when dreams and music come together.

As she looked ahead, Melanie knew that her journey was far from over. With each new project, she was excited to explore new dimensions of her artistry and to continue inspiring her fans to chase their own dreams. With the music as her guide, Melanie Martinez was ready to keep making magic, reminding the world that when dreams and music come alive, anything is possible.

Chapter 7: Sharing the Magic

As Melanie Martinez continued to rise in the music industry, she understood that the magic of her journey wasn't just meant for her, it was something to be shared with others. The stories, emotions, and experiences that inspired her songs were universal, and she felt a strong calling to connect with her fans on a deeper level. This connection was the heartbeat of her music and the essence of the magic she wanted to share.

From the very beginning, Melanie had always valued the bond she shared with her audience. She recognized that her fans were not just supporters; they were a community of dreamers, each carrying their own stories and struggles.

With this in mind, Melanie sought to create a space where everyone could feel seen, understood, and empowered. She wanted her concerts, her social media presence, and even her music to reflect this vision of inclusivity and support.

One of the most impactful ways Melanie shared the magic of her music was through her concerts. During her performances, she transformed the stage into a magical world where dreams could take flight. Each show was an immersive experience filled with dazzling visuals, theatrical elements, and heartfelt interactions. From the moment the lights dimmed and the first notes began to play, the audience was transported into Cry Baby's world. Melanie encouraged everyone to sing along, dance, and embrace their emotions, creating a collective atmosphere of joy and unity.

But it wasn't just the music that made her concerts special; it was the moments of connection she fostered with her fans. Melanie often took the time to speak to the audience, sharing personal stories and the inspiration behind her songs. She opened up about her own struggles, allowing her fans to see the real Melanie, an artist who faced challenges just like them. This vulnerability created a sense of trust and authenticity that resonated deeply with her audience.

In addition to her live performances, Melanie leveraged social media to maintain a close relationship with her fans. She used platforms like Instagram and Twitter to share snippets of her life, updates on new music, and messages of encouragement. She frequently engaged with her followers, responding to their comments and messages, and creating a dialogue that made them feel like they were part of her journey. Melanie wanted her fans to know that their voices mattered and that they were not alone in their struggles.

Another way Melanie shared the magic was through her creative projects. Whether it was her music videos, short films, or collaborations with other artists, each endeavor was infused with her signature style and storytelling. She often incorporated themes of self-acceptance, empowerment, and the importance of following your dreams, inspiring her audience to embrace their uniqueness. By sharing these messages through her art, Melanie encouraged her fans to find their own magic within.

One memorable example of sharing the magic was Melanie's initiative to involve her fans in her creative process. During the lead-up to her album releases, she often invited fans to participate in contests or challenges related to her music. Whether it was sharing their own artwork inspired by her songs or creating dance videos, these activities allowed her followers to express their creativity and connect with each other. This sense of community was a powerful reminder that they were all part of something larger, a movement fueled by dreams, music, and magic.

Melanie also understood the importance of using her platform for social good. She frequently spoke out on issues that mattered to her, such as mental health awareness, body positivity, and self-love. By sharing her own experiences and advocating for these causes, she inspired her fans to embrace their individuality and champion their own stories. Melanie believed that music had the power to heal, and she wanted her audience to know that it was okay to seek help and support when needed.

As she continued to grow as an artist, Melanie never lost sight of the magic that brought her fans together. She cherished the moments of connection, the shared emotions, and the stories that unfolded at her concerts and online. Each interaction reinforced the idea that music was a universal language a bridge that connected people from all walks of life.

Through her journey, Melanie Martinez became a beacon of hope and inspiration for her fans. She reminded them that their dreams were valid, that it was okay to feel deeply, and that they had the power to create their own magic. Sharing her story was about more than just her success; it was about fostering a community where everyone could feel empowered to be themselves.

As she looked toward the future, Melanie was excited to continue sharing the magic of her music and her journey. She knew that every song, every performance, and every interaction was an opportunity to inspire others and create a lasting impact. With each new chapter, Melanie Martinez would keep the magic alive, reminding her fans that together, they could dream big, embrace their uniqueness, and turn their dreams into reality.

Chapter 8: More Than Music

For Melanie Martinez, music was never just a career; it was a means of expression, a form of art, and a way to connect with others. As her journey continued to unfold, she realized that her influence extended far beyond the melodies and lyrics she created. The messages woven into her songs and the narratives portrayed in her videos represented something much deeper a platform for change, empowerment, and understanding.

Melanie understood that her music could spark conversations about important issues that many people faced but often felt too afraid to discuss. Throughout her career, she tackled themes like mental health, identity, and self-acceptance, recognizing that these topics were not just personal struggles but shared experiences for many of her fans. By bringing these subjects to the forefront, Melanie created a space for dialogue, encouraging her audience to embrace their vulnerabilities and seek help when needed.

One of the most significant aspects of Melanie's artistry was her commitment to authenticity. She often drew from her own life experiences, crafting songs that reflected the ups and downs of growing up. In doing so, she showed her fans that it was okay to feel confused, hurt, or lost feelings that are often stigmatized in society. By being open about her emotions, Melanie empowered her audience to express their own feelings, fostering a sense of community among those who resonated with her messages.

The song "Recess," for example, speaks directly to the pressures of youth and the need for a break from societal expectations. In it, Melanie addresses feelings of anxiety and the importance of taking time for oneself. The catchy chorus and playful beats invite listeners to dance, while the lyrics serve as a reminder to prioritize mental health. Through her music, she encouraged her fans to embrace their individuality and to remember that it's perfectly fine to step back and take a moment for themselves.

Moreover, Melanie's artistic vision extended beyond her music and into her fashion and visuals. Her distinctive style became a key component of her brand, symbolizing the whimsical yet poignant narratives she crafted. With vibrant colors, playful designs, and elements of nostalgia, Melanie's fashion choices complemented her music, creating a multi-layered artistic experience. Each outfit, music video, and performance was carefully curated to reflect her identity and the messages she wanted to convey.

Melanie also used her platform to support other artists and creators. She often collaborated with fellow musicians and encouraged her fans to uplift one another. By promoting creativity and sharing the spotlight, she fostered an environment where everyone could thrive. This sense of community was vital to Melanie, as she believed that collaboration breeds innovation and that every artist has a unique voice worth celebrating.

As her career progressed, Melanie continued to explore new avenues for expressing her artistry. She ventured into visual storytelling through her music videos and films, creating immersive experiences that captivated her audience. The short film accompanying her K-12 album was a testament to this evolution. It allowed her to tell a cohesive story through music, visuals, and performance, showcasing her talents as a filmmaker and storyteller. Through this medium, Melanie highlighted the importance of creativity and self-expression, encouraging her fans to explore their own artistic pursuits.

Moreover, Melanie became an advocate for body positivity and self-love, using her platform to challenge unrealistic beauty standards. In her song "Dollhouse," she explores the idea of perfection and the pressures to conform. By addressing these issues, she inspired her fans to embrace their flaws and appreciate their uniqueness. Melanie often emphasized that beauty comes in all forms, and that self-acceptance is a journey worth taking.

In addition to her music and artistry, Melanie recognized the importance of giving back. She actively supported various charities and initiatives that aligned with her values, particularly those focused on mental health awareness and youth empowerment. By using her influence for good, she aimed to create positive change in the world and inspire her fans to do the same.

In this way, Melanie Martinez became more than just a musician; she evolved into a role model and a source of inspiration for countless individuals. Through her authenticity, creativity, and commitment to important issues, she empowered her audience to embrace their true selves and pursue their passions. Her message was clear: music has the power to heal, connect, and inspire change, and it was a tool she would continue to wield with purpose.

As she looked toward the future, Melanie knew that her journey was far from over. With every new project, she aimed to explore the depths of her artistry and to continue using her platform for positive impact. She understood that music was just the beginning, her true mission was to create a world where everyone felt accepted, valued, and inspired to chase their dreams.

Through her passion and dedication, Melanie Martinez had woven a tapestry of music, art, and social change, reminding her fans that their voices matter and that they have the power to create their own magic. In a world where dreams sometimes feel out of reach, she stood as a testament to the belief that with hard work, authenticity, and a little bit of magic, anything is possible.

Chapter 9: Inspiring Young Dreamers

As Melanie Martinez's career blossomed, she recognized the incredible power of her influence on young people. She was aware that many of her fans looked up to her as a role model, and she felt a strong responsibility to inspire them to pursue their own dreams. With each song she wrote, every performance she delivered, and every story she shared, Melanie aimed to ignite a spark of creativity and determination within the hearts of young dreamers everywhere.

From the very beginning of her journey, Melanie had faced her own share of challenges. She understood that the path to success was often filled with obstacles, self-doubt, and the occasional setback. But through her music, she wanted to convey an important message: dreams are worth chasing, no matter how difficult the journey may seem. She wanted her young fans to know that it was okay to stumble and fall; what mattered most was getting back up and continuing to pursue what they loved.

One of the most powerful ways Melanie inspired young dreamers was through her lyrics. Many of her songs told stories of self-discovery, resilience, and embracing one's individuality. Tracks like "Pity Party" and "Sippy Cup" explored themes of heartache and vulnerability, reminding her audience that everyone experiences struggles. By openly sharing her feelings, Melanie created an environment where her fans could relate to her experiences and feel empowered to express their own emotions.

In her song "Play Date," Melanie highlighted the complexities of relationships, emphasizing that love can be both beautiful and confusing. This relatability resonated with her young audience, reminding them that they were not alone in their feelings. The message was clear: it's okay to feel deeply, and those feelings are valid. Through her music, Melanie encouraged her fans to embrace their emotions, fostering an environment of acceptance and understanding.

Melanie also utilized social media as a platform to connect with her fans directly. She frequently engaged with them, sharing snippets of her daily life, behind-the-scenes moments, and glimpses into her creative process. By allowing her audience to see the hard work and dedication that went into her art, she inspired them to pursue their passions, no matter how daunting the journey might seem. She wanted her young followers to understand that success doesn't come overnight; it takes perseverance, creativity, and a belief in oneself.

In addition to sharing her music, Melanie often encouraged her fans to express themselves creatively. She hosted contests where followers could submit their artwork, dance videos, or covers of her songs. By celebrating their talents and showcasing their creativity, she fostered a sense of community among her fans. This interaction not only inspired young dreamers to pursue their artistic passions but also created an environment where they felt valued and appreciated.

During her concerts, Melanie took the time to speak to her audience, sharing her personal story and the lessons she had learned along the way. She reminded her fans that their dreams were worth pursuing and that they should never be afraid to be themselves. Her uplifting words resonated deeply, filling her audience with hope and encouragement. Melanie wanted her young dreamers to leave her shows feeling inspired and ready to chase their aspirations.

One of the most memorable aspects of Melanie's influence was her dedication to promoting self-acceptance and self-love. In a world that often emphasizes perfection, she stood firm in her belief that everyone is unique and deserving of love just as they are. Through her music and public statements, she encouraged her fans to embrace their quirks, flaws, and individuality.

This powerful message was especially significant for young people navigating the complexities of growing up and finding their place in the world.

Melanie's commitment to supporting her fans extended beyond her music. She often partnered with organizations that focused on mental health awareness, body positivity, and youth empowerment. By using her platform to advocate for these causes, she not only inspired young dreamers but also encouraged them to be advocates for themselves and others. Melanie believed that every young person has the power to make a difference, and she wanted her fans to realize that they could use their voices for good.

As she continued her artistic journey, Melanie Martinez remained a beacon of inspiration for young dreamers around the globe. Her story was one of creativity, resilience, and authenticity, demonstrating that it's possible to turn dreams into reality with hard work and determination. She showed her fans that they are capable of achieving greatness and that their unique voices deserve to be heard.

In a world filled with challenges and uncertainties, Melanie's message of empowerment was a guiding light for young dreamers. She reminded them that their dreams are valid, their emotions matter, and that the magic of self-expression can change lives. Through her music, her words, and her unwavering support, Melanie Martinez inspired a generation to dream big, embrace their individuality, and chase their passions with courage and confidence.

As she looked ahead, Melanie knew that her mission was far from complete. She was excited to continue sharing her journey, uplifting her fans, and inspiring young dreamers to believe in themselves. After all, in the grand tapestry of life, everyone has a role to play and she was determined to help her audience find theirs. Through the power of music and the magic of dreams, Melanie Martinez would continue to inspire young hearts to reach for the stars.

Chapter 10: The Future's Melody

As Melanie Martinez looked ahead, she felt a sense of excitement and anticipation for what was to come. The journey that had begun with a dream was now a beautiful tapestry of music, art, and connection. With each step she took, Melanie was more determined than ever to continue creating, inspiring, and evolving. The future held endless possibilities, and she was ready to explore them all.

One of the things Melanie cherished most about her career was the ability to grow and experiment with her music. She had learned that every experience both joyful and challenging, shaped her artistry. With each album, she ventured into new sounds, styles, and themes, reflecting her evolving identity as an artist and a person. This growth was a natural part of her journey, and she embraced it wholeheartedly. As she looked toward the future, she envisioned a landscape filled with innovation, creativity, and exploration.

Melanie often imagined the kinds of music she wanted to create next. With her passion for storytelling and her love of connecting with her audience, she dreamt of crafting songs that would resonate deeply with listeners. She envisioned incorporating diverse musical influences, experimenting with different genres, and collaborating with artists from various backgrounds. These collaborations would not only enhance her sound but also serve as a reminder of the beauty of unity and collaboration in the creative process.

In her mind, the future's melody was a harmonious blend of the past and the present, a celebration of her journey, her growth, and her dreams. She saw it as an opportunity to delve into new themes and ideas that mattered to her and her audience. Topics such as empowerment, mental health, and the importance of self-love would continue to be central to her music. With each note, she hoped to inspire and uplift her fans, encouraging them to embrace their own unique journeys.

Beyond music, Melanie envisioned expanding her artistic expression into new mediums. She had always loved storytelling, and she dreamed of creating more visual projects, such as short films and animated stories that accompanied her music. Through these projects, she aimed to transport her audience to new worlds filled with imagination and emotion. She wanted to explore different narratives, bringing her songs to life through captivating visuals that convey powerful messages.

Additionally, Melanie recognized the importance of continuing to foster a sense of community among her fans. She wanted to create spaces where young dreamers could connect, share their stories, and support one another. By encouraging dialogue and collaboration, she hoped to inspire a generation to embrace their individuality and pursue their passions fearlessly.

Melanie also dreamed of using her platform for even greater impact. She envisioned partnering with organizations focused on mental health, youth empowerment, and the arts to promote awareness and create positive change. By combining her love for music with her desire to make a difference, she hoped to leave a lasting legacy that would inspire future generations to dream big and believe in themselves.

With every new project, Melanie aspired to create a ripple effect of positivity and inspiration. She wanted her fans to feel empowered to share their own stories, to use their voices, and to embrace their creativity. The future's melody would be one of hope, encouragement, and connection to a beautiful symphony where everyone had a part to play.

As she continued to write and create, Melanie found herself inspired by the stories of her fans. She often received messages from young dreamers sharing their own journeys, struggles, and triumphs. These stories filled her with joy and reminded her of the power of music to connect people. In the future, she hoped to incorporate more of these real-life experiences into her work, crafting songs that resonated with her audience on a personal level.

The future's melody was not just about Melanie's journey; it was about all the dreamers who looked up to her. She wanted her music to be a source of comfort and empowerment for those navigating their own paths. In her heart, she believed that every individual has a unique melody waiting to be expressed, and she felt honored to be a part of that journey.

As she stepped into the next chapter of her career, Melanie Martinez embraced the unknown with open arms. She knew that the future was full of possibilities, and she was excited to explore them all. With each note she wrote and every story she told, she would continue to inspire young dreamers to chase their passions, celebrate their uniqueness, and create their own melodies.

The future's melody was a beautiful reminder that dreams are not only meant to be pursued but also shared. Melanie's journey was just beginning, and she was determined to make every moment count. Through her music, her creativity, and her unwavering spirit, she would continue to inspire others to find their own magic and sing their own songs. The future was bright, and the melody was waiting to be composed of a symphony of dreams, love, and limitless possibilities.

CONCLUSION

As we reach the end of Melanie Martinez's inspiring journey, it's clear that her story is not just about a girl who became a pop star; it's about a dreamer who turned her visions into reality through passion, creativity, and resilience. From her humble beginnings in New York to captivating audiences worldwide, Melanie has shown us that dreams are possible, no matter how big or small.

Throughout her career, Melanie has used her music as a powerful tool for expression, touching the hearts of countless fans. Her songs resonate with themes of self-acceptance, mental health, and individuality, inviting listeners to embrace their own stories and emotions. She has transformed her experiences both joyful and challenging, into beautiful melodies that inspire young dreamers to chase their aspirations, no matter the obstacles they may face.

Melanie's journey also highlights the importance of authenticity. She reminds us that being true to ourselves is the key to finding our unique voices. Through her whimsical visuals and captivating performances, she encourages her fans to celebrate their individuality and express themselves freely. She believes that every person has a story worth telling and a melody waiting to be sung, and she inspires young dreamers to believe in their own magic.

In addition to her music, Melanie's commitment to creating a supportive community has left a lasting impact. By encouraging her fans to connect, share, and uplift one another, she has fostered an environment where creativity thrives. Through her advocacy for mental health and body positivity, she has empowered countless individuals to embrace their true selves and pursue their passions with confidence.

As we look to the future, we know that Melanie Martinez's journey is far from over. With her creativity and determination, she will continue to inspire generations of young dreamers to follow their hearts and create their own paths. Her story is a reminder that dreams are not just fantasies; they can become reality with hard work, dedication, and a sprinkle of magic.

So, to all the young dreamers reading this book, remember: your dreams matter. Embrace your unique journey, let your voice be heard, and never be afraid to shine. Like Melanie, you have the power to turn your dreams into magic. The world is waiting for your melody, go out and create it!

Made in the USA
Las Vegas, NV
23 November 2024

12470217R00046